SCRAMBLED STARTS

Family Prayers for Morning, Bedtime, and Everything In-Between

JENNY YOUNGMAN

UPPER ROOM BOOKS®
NASHVILLE

Upper Room Books® website: books.upperroom.org

Upper Room®, Upper Room Books®, and design logos are trademarks owned by The Upper Room®, a ministry of GBOD®, Nashville, Tennessee. All rights reserved.

All scripture quotations are from the Common English Bible. Copyright © 2011 Common English Bible. Used by permission.

Cover and interior design, hand-lettering, and illustration: Jay Smith / Juicebox Designs

Library of Congress Cataloging-in-Publication Data

Youngman, Jenny.
  Scrambled starts : family prayers for morning, bedtime, and everything in-between / Jenny Youngman.
      pages cm
  ISBN 978-0-8358-1499-7 (print)—ISBN 978-0-8358-1537-6 (mobi)—978-0-8358-1500-0 (epub)
1. Families—Prayers and devotions. I. Title.
  BV255.Y68 2015
  249—dc23

                                    2015001129

Printed in the United States of America

CONTENTS

PREFACE

When you chose to grab this book off the shelf or read the sample pages online, you might have made assumptions about me that I need to clear up from the start. As a reader, I reach for a book from the Upper Room because I expect a certain level of expertise and experience from their authors. I expect to be confronted by the Holy Spirit and feel my heart transformed. Many Upper Room books have shaped me theologically and shaped my daily spiritual practice. Their Spiritual Classics series has provided a treasure trove for my searching soul.

When Upper Rooms Books invited me into their ranks, I must confess that I joined them with a sense of awe and gratitude. I am not an expert in prayer or parenting or faith-formed families or anything for that matter. (Sorry if that is what you were looking for!) For the sake of full disclosure, you should know that I am simply a mom who is desperate to co-lead with my husband a family of spiritually deep, praying kids who believe with all their hearts that God not only hears their prayers but also stands ready to answer. I believe that prayer will bind my family together when our schedules and commitments have us running in every direction. I believe that prayer is the thing that will bind my kids' hearts to God's heart when the world around them begs for their allegiance. I believe that prayer is how our broken hearts will find healing, where our hurtful words will find forgiveness, and where our need for second and third and fourth chances will find grace. I believe that prayer is at the heart of a faith-filled family.

I believe these things, yet my own family is still learning and growing into this identity. Since we do not measure our prayer lives with charts and numbers, the only way to know if our prayer lives are thriving is by praying and then waiting to see the prayers answered.

My young family finds itself in this season of waiting. My husband, children, and I gather every morning around our breakfast table, and sometimes we have meaningful prayers and conversations. Sometimes we are hurried and hollering. Sometimes our prayers are monotonous, laborious, and random. But we keep gathering anyway with full assurance that God will hear the prayers of our hearts even if our words don't come out quite right. In fact, we anticipate that God will act and answer our prayers, so we wait to see the hand of God at work among us. It is an awesome thing—praying, waiting, and witnessing the answered prayers. I pray that you will find hope or help or a new idea among these pages. I pray God's richest blessing upon you and your family as you grow together through prayer.

ACKNOWLEDGMENTS

I am grateful for my husband, Mark Youngman, who is also my pastor. He teaches me, prays with and for me, and answers all our kids' big faith questions with grace and commitment. I thank God for my precious kids, Gracie, Myles, Olivia, and Beckett. Their prayers for me are sweet and encouraging, and I praise God for their tender hearts.

I am also thankful for my editors, Jeannie Crawford-Lee and Joanna Bradley, who took my idea seriously and who I duped into believing that I could write a book that belonged on the shelves next to my modern faith heroes.

And finally, thank you, Lord, for the gift of conversation with you. Thank you for beginning a good work in me and for your unwavering faithfulness to bring it to completion. To you alone be the glory.

INTRODUCTION

Gathered around the Sunday school table, glue sticks and construction-paper crafts strewn about, my teacher would announce, "It's time to pray, class. Would someone like to volunteer?" As all my friends shuffled their papers and hoped to remain unnoticed, I raised my little hand knowing my effort would win me a smile and a welcome affirmation. And it always did.

"Dear Jesus," I would pray, "thank you for this day and thank you for my teacher. Forgive us for our sins and help us to be nice. In Jesus' name I pray. Amen."

Proud of myself, I would leave for worship ready to prove my childhood piety even more by closing my eyes and raising my hands during the hymns and worship songs. In my tradition, leading prayers and exhibiting signs of participation during worship served as outward expressions of committed believers, and I wanted to be one of them!

Somewhere between childhood and the teenage years, my confidence to pray grew even more, but the prayers became more legalistic in nature. At night I would regularly mutter out a quick prayer asking forgiveness while nodding off to sleep just to be sure that I was still "good with God." The "If I die before I wake" notion had been so sealed into my understanding of faith that I feared what might happen if I did in fact die before morning came.

Though my young prayers may have had occasionally misguided motives, I realize now that every attempt at prayer was a step toward God. I discovered in my childhood prayers and piety that even though I didn't really know how to pray and was not always genuine in my approach, I was practicing prayer. I was doing it! Going through the motions at a young age taught me how to pray as I grew up. The practice of prayer taught me the language that I could come back to again and again.

GROWING UP IN PRAYER

Prayer drew me in at a young age with its mystery, wonder, and power. That God Almighty would incline an ear to me seemed magical and wonderful. I have always loved the idea that God listens to me, wants to speak to me, and waits for me to share my heart. Through prayer, faith grows, love for God grows, and our beliefs mature. In time, I began to understand prayer more holistically. I realized that prayer is less a give-and-take exchange with God and more a two-way conversation between the Creator of the universe and God's beloved child—me.

Prayer became so much more than a holy pass that wiped my sin slate clean or a tool to show off my spirituality or even a rehearsal of my glorified Christmas list. Prayer became my very breath, taking in the Spirit of God and breathing out the anxieties, fears, and pain of the world. I grew to understand prayer as a beautiful exchange between a God who knows what I need and me—God's beloved creation—who brings forward my needs anyway.

My desire for a deeper prayer life led me to classical writings on prayer, the prayers of the saints, and the practice of silence, solitude, and breath prayers. In seminary, my studies revolved around spiritual disciplines and prayer practices. My prayer journey has led me to teach, write, and lead retreats on prayer practices. The practice of prayer never lets me go; in fact, I often feel a tangible hunger for time spent with God in prayer.

ATTEMPTS AT FAMILY PRAYER

Early in our marriage, my husband, Mark, and I would often read a book of the Bible together and pray about our future and what God had in store for us. We would hold hands and commit our dreams to God, asking for God's will to be planted in our hearts. We'd share with each other the ways that scripture was soaking into our thoughts and actions. As we moved into local church ministry and began a family, I believed that prayer would be the focus of our home life and that our children would know how and when and why to pray before they even knew how to talk.

But here is the truth: Despite my journey with prayer, my experience, and my education, I have found creating a pattern of prayer for my family to be awkward at best and

11

excruciating at worst. As most newlyweds do, Mark and I made assumptions about how our family would operate when it was time for kids. I held grandiose beliefs about the spiritual life of our family. We would be, or so I dreamed, a family that prayed aloud together, memorized scriptures, and refused to get on the hurry-and-worry train of kids' activities. I just couldn't buy into the idea that families must be overscheduled, exhausted, and spiritually stuck. I was sure that our family would be different. My husband was a pastor after all; surely we had a leg up on the spiritual life!

Well, it didn't come together as easily as I thought it might. Turns out that family schedules can go haywire fairly quickly, and fatigue sucks out all creativity and good intentions. Commitments begin to pile up, and often bedtime and mealtime are the only family gatherings during the week, and even those are sporadic.

Beyond the constant struggle with my family's daily schedule, I was most surprised to discover that I lacked confidence in teaching my own children how to pray. It wasn't only about finding the time. Even the words came slowly and awkwardly as I attempted to pray with them. My words felt forced and labored. Out of fatigue, laziness, or fear, I often found it painful to gather my children for family prayer time. Of course, I prayed for them in my personal prayer time, but we were clumsy (to say the least) in our prayers together.

Prayer time can be awkward because kids are kids. They get distracted and transition from prayer to a recitation of their Christmas lists and back again. Or—and this is my favorite—they place every stuffed animal they own on the prayer list. Or they hope every single person they know has a good day. I've often wondered if it's even worth the effort.

But I choose to offer myself grace and remember that my children too are learning the language of prayer much like I did as a child. They are discovering how to bring before God the needs in their hearts and how to trust God with their desires and hopes. They are learning to place others (even their stuffed friends) before God and trust God with their care. These motions set a foundation for what will become their future prayer lives.

At our house, my children, husband, and I sing a blessing before meals, and we have morning devotions every day before school. These efforts are faith-filled and oftentimes lovely. But still I desire a more thriving family prayer life—one less hurried and more intentional. How I long for my family to pray together as easily as we laugh together. I am desperate for my children to learn to pray, to fall on their knees before God with all of their needs, desires, questions, hopes, and pleadings. I want them to search God's heart as I do, to crave time with God as I do, and to learn to listen for God's voice as I am learning to listen. I want them to volunteer to pray for their friends who might be hurt or struggling. I want to lead a pace of life slow enough for them to feel a margin—to have enough free time to think, dream, and hope.

TRIAL AND ERROR

My family's morning devotion time came about after I'd had enough of our crazy morning routine that involved one too many snooze buttons, kids running every which way, breakfast food hurled at the table, lunch food tossed into bags, lots of screaming at one another, and often a few tears thrown in for good measure. My husband and I decided to introduce morning devotions and prayer time at the table into our routine. Of course this would mean waking up earlier, which would also mean going to bed earlier the night before. It meant packing lunches the night before and having a plan for breakfast before walking into the kitchen at zero-dark-thirty. It meant less hurry and more intention.

My family has fumbled through the first year of morning devotions before school, and it now feels routine. The kids expect a Bible reading, a worship song, and prayer time before we are off on our way for the day. Some days we match the picture in my head of what I think is supposed to happen. Other days we are all at a loss for words in prayer, we have no time for song, and the sound of crunching cereal drowns out the Bible story. We are not perfect, but we are practicing. I believe when it comes to the spiritual life, practice makes practice—not perfect. We train our kids, we train ourselves, and eventually we find a stride.

I wrote this book because of my exasperation with failed attempts at family prayer, yet I'm hopeful that God will form our hearts and bless our attempts. I wrote these prayers for my family and for yours so that we have common words to speak. I wrote these prayers to teach us how to pray when the words don't come easily. My hope is that by memorizing or reading these prayers aloud, we will learn the language of prayer so that we may learn to pray freely, spontaneously, and on our own.

Wherever you are on your family's prayer journey, I hope that this book will be a tool to help you learn to pray together and that God will answer your prayers with more than you could have ever asked for or imagined.

HOW TO USE THE PRAYERS AND DEVOTIONS

Feel free to jump into this book and start wherever you find a natural entry point for your family. Maybe you immediately imagine a morning routine of prayer or devotions. Or maybe you want to set the book on the dinner table and let the kids choose a mealtime prayer. Maybe you want to try the practice of Examen at bedtime. The chapters are divided into categories so that you can start anywhere.

You may find a few prayers that you'd like your family to memorize and pray together at meals or other times. In that case, you may want to make a poster with the prayer for a reference.

This book is meant to be a resource for parents who need both encouragement for family prayer and the words to say. I hope that a common language will give roots to a life of prayer so that it becomes part of your family language.

Blessings on your journey in prayer!

CHAPTER
ONE
Mealtime
Prayers.

While they were eating, Jesus took bread, blessed it, broke it, and gave it to his disciples and said, "Take and eat."
—MATTHEW 26:26

Hurry poisons modern family life. It brings about the death of regular family gatherings, home-cooked meals, and lingering at the table. We race from work to get the kids, head home to make the "quick and easy" recipe for dinner, eat without any conversation, then run to dance or soccer or church. There's no time to be thankful!

Preparing food together, setting the table, gathering, and holding hands in prayer has given way to fast food eaten in the car prefaced by "Thank you, Jesus!" prayers said more out of duty than gratitude. Yet we long for slower, more intentional conversations with family around a dinner table.

Feeling tired from the frantic rush of my life, I decided to meet with a wise friend and spiritual director to sort out my frustrations. I had been worrying about whether to quit working, work less, or do something different altogether. I was tired of fighting the battle between family time and work. I kept coming back to the conclusion that I couldn't quit because who would do my job if I wasn't there to do it? Surely the whole company would go bankrupt in a matter of minutes. Maybe the building might even collapse as I drove away.

My friend kindly looked me straight in the eyes and told me that I was confused. She suggested that perhaps I had let myself believe that I was so important to the company that it couldn't survive without me and that might be just a wee bit of an exaggeration. She suggested that perhaps I was being a little full of myself.

Let's be honest with ourselves. Can't we call our manic running every which way what it is—self-indulgence? We make everything urgent and important. We tell ourselves, *If I'm not there to get it done, who will do it? Will it be done correctly?* We wonder how our children will get accepted into college if they don't take part in every possible extracurricular activity. We confuse busyness with importance. And maybe, just maybe, we are too full of ourselves.

We forget that the important things are done slowly, intentionally—spending time with friends, listening to our kids, choosing slow family meals over grab-and-go. It is nearly impossible to be grateful when we fill our schedules so tightly that we only have time to spit out a quick word between bites of our value meals. Do we believe that the world will fall apart if we slow down to share a meal and pray with our families?

Sometimes I am able to readjust my routine to allow more time at the dinner table with my family, but sometimes I am stuck with a crazy schedule for a season. When everyone in my family is pursuing a passion at exactly the same time, the combined stress level elevates. In the midst of our busyness, we have to practice intentionality in giving thanks for our meals wherever and whenever they are shared.

Mealtime becomes the time and space for family prayer. Even if just for a moment, mealtime prayers get everyone on the same page as a family.

GRATITUDE AS A FAMILY VALUE

Praying before meals fills our hearts with gratitude for God's provision in our lives as we enjoy the tangible gifts of food. We acknowledge that every good thing comes from God. We ask God to bless our food, bless the ones who prepared it, and bless the receivers of the goodness. We pray before meals to invite God's presence into our lives and to ask that the food become strength for our work in the kingdom.

The family dinner table serves as the primary location where children learn the importance of prayer in a family. How would your kids describe your family's current mealtime prayer routine? Do you pray at every meal? Do you sing the same blessing each meal? Do you share the duty of giving thanks? Or do you grab your food and head to the TV room? Children learn about the significance of prayer by watching how intentional their parents are about it. You claim mealtime as a sacred time by stopping what you're doing to turn your heart toward God in thanksgiving.

Some of the most important work of parenting is naming things for our kids. We get to declare certain ideas as fact: Fire is hot; ice is cold; cars go fast. In the work of naming, we can also shape priorities and values. When we claim that God is our strength, we are pointing to a family value. The

21

meal isn't the strength, but through it the Provider gives us strength through nourishment. The gathering together isn't the strength, but the Companion gives us strength in the meeting. When we make prayers around the table a priority, we name and claim that God is the source of our strength and that God is the one to be thanked and praised.

THE PRACTICE OF MEALTIME PRAYERS

Mealtime prayers are perhaps the most obvious entry point for families to begin a prayer life. When my kids were in preschool, they learned the prayer song "God, Our Father." It was set to the tune of "Frère Jacques" or "Brother John," and my family adopted the song as the table blessing for our home as well. Through the years, the kids have changed the rhythm, added some clapping, and attempted singing in a round, but they learned to pray by repeating that song three times a day for several years. Now that my oldest daughter is approaching the teenage years, she has outgrown the singsong approach. But because my children's ages span from six to twelve, we have started sharing leadership of the blessing so everyone gets a chance to choose the prayer.

In the early years, repetition is key. The same song every meal, even at restaurants or in the car, helps the practice become a habit. I've found that if I forget to begin the prayer, my kids remember to say it without my instruction. And soon enough, they are each clamoring to be the prayer leader!

Some of the prayers that follow are singsong, some rhyme for memorization, and others are simply written prayers to be read aloud by a parent or child. A different family member may be assigned a day to choose and lead the prayer. Don't wait for the "right time" to begin a mealtime prayer routine. The next time your family eats together, jump in and everyone else will most likely join!

Let the morning bring us word of your unfailing love, O Lord.
Receive our praise as we greet this day.
Bless this meal and give us strength
To share your love along the way. Amen.

Thank you, Lord, for our night of rest.
Come join our table and be our guest.
Bless the food that is prepared.
May it give us strength to follow you everywhere. Amen.

[sung to the tune of "Frère Jacques"]
God our Father (God our Father)
Once again (Once again)
We bow our heads and thank you
(We bow our heads and thank you)
Amen (Amen).
—TRADITIONAL

God is great. God is good.
Let us thank him for our food.
By God's hands we are fed.
Thank you Lord, for daily bread. Amen.
—TRADITIONAL

Thank you for the world so sweet.
Thank you for the food we eat.
Thank you for the birds that sing.
Thank you, God, for everything.
—AUTHOR UNKNOWN

Thank you, Lord, for this good food
And for the hands that made it.
Thank you, Lord, that you care for us
And join us at this table. Amen.

Gracious God, we give you thanks for all you are and
all you have done for us. This meal before us reminds us
of your provision and care. Let this food sustain us as
we go about the day in love. Amen.

Lord Jesus Christ, be present at our table. We invite
you now, Lord, to fellowship and feast with us as we
gather in your name. Amen.

Heavenly Father, we gather around this table to be renewed, encouraged, and strengthened. We are ever grateful that you are our Provider. Receive our humble gift of thanks for all you are and have done. Amen.

Lord, be praised by our gathering around this meal. We come with gratitude in our hearts and thanksgiving on our lips for the gifts set before us. May we know your joy and experience your love as we feast and fellowship together. Amen.

Thank you, Lord, for these your wonderful gifts and for the beautiful hands that prepared them. May this meal strengthen us to do whatever work you have set before us. Equip us for your service through Christ our Lord. Amen.

For each new morning with its light,
For rest and shelter of the night,
For health and food, for love and friends,
For everything Thy goodness sends,
Father in heaven, we thank you.
—AUTHOR UNKNOWN[1]

Bless, O Lord, your gifts to our use and us to your
service for Christ's sake. Amen.
—ADAPTED FROM THE BOOK OF COMMON PRAYER

Though we are rushed and eating fast,
We pause now before the meal has passed.
We know all good gifts come from you.
We thank you for our family and for this food. Amen.

Praise God, from whom all blessings flow;
Praise him, all creatures here below;
Praise him above, ye heavenly host;
Praise Father, Son, and Holy Ghost. Amen.
—TRADITIONAL DOXOLOGY

CHAPTER TWO

Bedtime Prayers

Only in God do I find rest;
my salvation comes from him.
Only God is my rock and my salvation—
my stronghold!—I won't be shaken anymore.
—PSALM 62:1-2

When babies are born into a family, every moment is precious. We take countless photos, document every burp and giggle, and stare in awe as our sweet little ones sleep. As they grow, bedtime routines become, well, a little more like a circus than a lullaby. Toddlers play catch me if you can, kids ask for just one more book, and teenagers beg for a later curfew. By the time our kids are actually tucked in tight, we are exhausted and out of energy. We may find it difficult to take that one extra breath and prolong bedtime just a few more minutes to pray together.

In truth, this is probably my biggest struggle in my quest to become a power-praying family. I can sing the song; I can read the book. But adding the prayer to that mix at the end of a long day spent driving between school, activities, church, meetings, and errands, and I am at a loss for words.

Sadly, I confess that my oldest child gets the least of me at bedtime. She gets a quick review of the day, a rundown of the next day's needs, and kiss on the forehead. But in the quiet and stillness of their rooms—the babies and the big kids—how I long for prayerful moments and grace-filled conversations, thanking God for the day and inviting rest and peace. I'm working on this one, knowing full well that the adolescent years are the most important season to model spiritual practices so they become habits as the teenagers transition to adulthood.

BEYOND "IF I DIE BEFORE I WAKE"

I bet we all said this prayer as children: "Now I lay me down to sleep. I pray the Lord my soul to keep. If I die before I wake, I pray the Lord my soul to take." While I understand the sentiment, there's something about ending the day focused on death that unsettles me. I want my kids to rest well, assured that their futures in heaven are safe and secure because of the work of Jesus on the cross and his invitation of love in their lives. I'd rather they boldly claim that promise instead of making a timid request each night just to be safe.

I'd rather look back on a day with my kids and celebrate all that God has done, recount the places where we saw God, invite God's peace into our hearts as we rest, and place tomorrow into God's care. "If I die before I wake" can cause a "Just in case I'm not right with God, I better get this in" mindset when God has made us right already. God has claimed us, promised us a future in heaven, and empowered us to live with joy instead of fear.

THE PRACTICE OF EXAMEN

One of the spiritual practices I have come to love is the practice of Examen, or a prayerful examination of the

32

day. The practice comes from Saint Ignatius of Loyola, a sixteenth-century mystic and the founder of the Jesuit order of priests. He believed this form of prayer to be one of the most important, and he saw it as a gift of God to be practiced regularly. Even today, Jesuit priests are instructed to pray the Examen twice a day: once at noon and again at the close of the day.

In this prayer practice, you focus and reflect on the awareness of God's presence throughout the day. You ask questions such as, Where did I see God today?, At what points in the day did I feel far from God?, How did I experience joy today?, and What made me sad today?

In a similar way, John Wesley, the reformer and leader of the Methodist movement, invited his small bands of Jesus-followers to ask one another, "How is it with your soul?" I love the idea of inviting children to explore the state of their souls at bedtime. Are they happy? Are they joy-filled? Are they worried about something at school? Are they mad at their siblings? Are they grateful for their blessings? Are they disappointed about a decision they made during the day? Were they too rushed and hurried?

Notice the contrast in language between the Examen questions and "If I die before I wake, I pray the Lord my soul to take." Giving them language to explore what is going on in their hearts and souls and how they might invite God to heal, forgive, nurture, encourage, and help them goes far beyond making sure they'll get to heaven each night. What

33

a privilege it is as parents to encourage kids' awareness of God's movement in their lives!

SADS, GLADS, AND SORRYS

My friend Kara Oliver uses a mealtime routine with her family that I loved so much I stole it for my kids' bedtime—and I'm stealing it again to share in this book. She calls it Sads, Glads, and Sorrys.[2] Each family member names anything he or she is sad about, glad about, or sorry for. In a way, this is another form of Examen—looking back on the day and observing our walk with God. The practice of reflecting on high points, low points, God sightings, joys, sins, needs, worries, and hopes teaches our kids to bring everything before God with gratitude and full assurance that God hears them, is with them, and will answer their prayers. What a gift for growing hearts!

HOW TO START A BEDTIME PRAYER ROUTINE

Remember how I said I'm pretty much a failure at bedtime prayers? Well that's still true. I know how important and meaningful it can be to pray with my kids at bedtime, but I often lack the follow-through to make it happen. So let's challenge ourselves right now to be intentional about our families' prayer life and make bedtime prayers a priority.

In theory, my family has a bedtime routine that goes as follows (that is, when everyone is miraculously at home in the evenings to make it happen): bath, pajamas, book, prayer, song. Admittedly, I frequently skip the prayer and sing the song while handing out good-night kisses and walking out the door. Most days are long and exhausting, and I'm ready to get to the couch to put my feet up and enjoy some grown-up conversation. I'm convicted even as I write this that a few more minutes, slowed down and unhurried, to prayerfully reflect on the day with my kids is a gift all of us would enjoy.

So how do you start bedtime prayers? The answer is that you just start doing it. Sometimes it's helpful to post the morning and bedtime routines in the hallway so everyone in the family is on the same page. The more you keep a routine, the more the practice is likely to stick.

QUESTIONS FOR EXAMEN
Where did you see God today?
What moments did you wish had lasted longer?
What moments seemed to drag on?
What do you wish you could change about today?
When did you feel God's presence today?
When did you have to depend on God today?
What made you sad today?
What made you glad today?
What are you sorry for that happened today?

After exploring some questions of Examen, give thanks to God for the day. Invite God's healing, forgiveness, or encouragement where needed. Ask God for a peaceful sleep and strength for tomorrow.

Jesus, tender Shepherd, hear me,
Bless thy little lamb tonight;
Through the darkness be Thou near me,
Watch my sleep til morning light.
—MARY DUNCAN

PATRICK'S EVENING HYMN[3]

O Christ, Son of the Living God,
May your holy angels guard our sleep.
May they watch us as we rest
and hover around our beds.

Let them reveal to us in our dreams
Visions of your glorious truth,
O High Prince of the universe,
O High Priest of the mysteries.

May no dreams disturb our rest
And no nightmares darken our dreams.
May no fears or worries delay
Our willing, prompt response.

May the virtue of our daily work
Hallow our nightly prayers.
May our sleep be deep and soft,
So our work may be fresh and hard.

Thank you Lord, for this good day.
Help us now to sleep, we pray.
And in our rest, please grant us strength
To serve you well in work and play.

The LORD bless you and protect you.
The LORD make his face shine on you and be gracious
to you.
The LORD lift up his face to you and grant you peace.
—NUMBERS 6:24-26

God, we are ever grateful for your great love and care.
Thank you for the blessings of this day.
Forgive us our sins and give us grace.
Hold our hearts as we rest this night.
Wake us tomorrow to follow you wherever you may
lead. Amen.

Now I lay me down to sleep,
I pray, O Lord, my heart to keep.
Watch over my family and my friends,
And wake us with sunshine when nighttime ends.

Deep peace of the running wave to you.
Deep peace of the flowing air to you.
Deep peace of the quiet earth to you.
Deep peace of the shining stars to you.

Deep peace of the gentle night to you.
Moon and stars pour their healing light on you.
Deep peace of Christ,
of Christ the light of the world to you.
Deep peace of Christ to you.
—TRADITIONAL GAELIC BLESSING

THE JESUS PRAYER

Lord Jesus Christ, Son of God, have mercy on me,
a sinner.

CHAPTER
THREE

Morning
Devotions

Tell me all about your faithful love come morning time,
because I trust you.
Show me the way I should go,
because I offer my life up to you.
—PSALM 143:8

Recently I flinched when I read that most moral and spiritual foundations are locked in place by age nine.[4] That means our kids' soft, mushy, play-dough hearts set to a more solid form before they turn ten. After age nine or so, kids begin to test any new information against their previously formed foundations. They begin to make sense of the world around them by judging everything from their moral and spiritual baseline. As parents, we better be intentional about building that foundation in our children's early years.

Not surprisingly, just getting kids to church on Sundays doesn't necessarily set that solid foundation from which spiritually mature adults will grow. Sociologist of religion Robert Wuthnow claims, "It is religious training in the home that appears to [best predict adult church attendance]: family devotions as a child are the best preceptor of adult attendance, followed by seeing one's parents read the Bible at home, and after that, by parents having read the Bible to the child."[5] Going to church regularly is a part of spiritually training children, but it is not the singular practice that will give our kids a foundation of faith.

Christian families serve as house churches where parents are the pastors, the chaplains, and the Christian educators. When we go to church as a family, the goal is not to disperse into separate hallways for our one-hour-a-week instruction taught by professionals. We go to church together to gather with the saints and because we are part of something greater. Sure, we learn from studied Bible teachers and hear a word from a credentialed and called pastor, but the church isn't meant to be the one point of spiritual contact our kids have in a week. Family worship, whether morning, noon, or night, speaks volumes to our kids about what a family values and about a Christian worldview. It also helps set a pattern of spiritual discipline that kids will follow into adulthood.

SCRAMBLED STARTS

For some reason, intentional morning devotions have come a little easier for my family than other opportunities for family prayer. Maybe because of the time of day—schedules have yet to get off-track. Or maybe it's because the gathering is not dependent on my words but the scriptures, songs, and corporate prayers instead.

For the first few years my kids were in school, mornings began like an impending tornado. The siren (alarm) sounded louder and louder until everyone was up and running around in full crisis mode. *Where are my shoes? You're taking too long in the bathroom! Stop hitting your sister! My socks hate me! I hate oatmeal!•We're late! Get in the car!*

44

Sound familiar? It only took me a few years of this craziness to decide to do something about it. Feeling convicted about the spirit of hurry and anger with which my family members began their days, I prayed for an idea that would change us, that would send us out with peace and encouragement rather than worry and upset hearts.

After perusing Pinterest and various blogs for ideas, I developed a morning routine that worked for my family. We wake up with ample time to get ready for the day and meet at the breakfast table thirty minutes before we have to leave for school. For thirty minutes, we eat breakfast, talk about what the day has in store, read a Bible story, sing a worship song, and pray together. The first time we followed through with our new routine, we all agreed that this was a much better way to start the day. We even had extra time to get out the door. We had time to see that our bags were well packed. We had time to hug and say encouraging words to one another. What a difference that morning made! Now we are starting our second year of morning worship; it's both a routine and a welcomed expectation of every morning.

My favorite change about organizing a morning routine to include family worship is that it starts the day with love. Though we love each other deeply, my family's previous morning routine did not display that affection and, in fact, brought out the worst in all of us. Now we start the day with love, which is the foundation I want my children to stand on. I want them to know how loved they are—by their father, by me, and by their God. I want them to know that as a family, we cheer for one another every day when we walk out the door. I want to surround them with love so that they know who and whose they are when the day gets confusing.

CHANGING HABITS

In order to make morning worship happen, everyone in the family has to make some changes of habit. If the morning routine is going to be altered to create more time, that means the evening routine will need some adaptations as well. In theory, when we are not out at ball games or school events, my family and I are home and in the bedtime routine by seven o'clock. The younger children are asleep by seven thirty, followed by the older ones at eight o'clock and eight thirty. Now for the hard part—getting Mom and Dad to sleep!

After a long day, sometimes my husband and I just want to plop onto the couch and turn on the TV. We know we should just go to bed, but for some reason we call this quality time together. We had to agree that this was not our best effort, and we put aside the late nights. It takes surprising discipline to turn off the TV at night instead of staying up for the news or the talk shows. But when he and I get enough sleep, we wake up with more energy and are able to set a tone of grace, space, and kindness.

HOW TO BEGIN FAMILY MORNING WORSHIP

For my family, beginning morning worship meant creating a routine and following it every single day. The alarms go off at the same time. We get out of bed after hitting the snooze button only once. My husband and I get ready for the day. We wake up the kids, and they have thirty minutes to get ready and get to the table. Once at the table, we pass around the breakfast food and talk about what is going on that day. Then we read from a storybook Bible or children's devotional book, sing a worship song together, and finally each of us takes a turn in prayer. I love the way we greet the day together, commit any of our worries to God, and invite God to shine through us during the day.

If you're considering beginning morning worship, spend a few minutes reflecting on your current morning routine. What is the tone at your house every morning? How do you and your kids feel when you walk out the door for the day? What would it take to create a little more space for family worship time? Write down some possible routines that would work for you, starting with your wake-up time.

Remember that everything you do in training your kids in the way of faith sets a foundation from which they will grow. I've written some morning devotions in the next few pages to help you get started, but feel free to do what suits your time, your kids, and your personality. Create the space for family worship, and let the Holy Spirit be your guide.

RISE AND SHINE

Ask someone to read Psalm 19:1 aloud: "Heaven is declaring God's glory; the sky is proclaiming his handiwork."

Sing or listen to a favorite worship song or hymn.

Read the Creation story from a Bible storybook. My personal favorite is *The Jesus Storybook Bible* by Sally Lloyd Jones but use what you have. If you don't have a storybook Bible, take turns reading Genesis 1:1–2:4 from any Bible.

After the Bible story, ask, "What do we hear God saying to us in this story?" Declare that you are all created by God and called good by the Creator of the whole universe! Celebrate that no matter what happens throughout the day, you are created, known, and loved by God.

Ask for prayer requests. They can be anything—help for tests, friends who are ill, gratitude for teachers, and so on. Close by praying together, making sure each person gets an opportunity to pray aloud.

NOTHING CAN SEPARATE US

Ask someone to read Psalm 139:7-10 aloud: "Where could I go to get away from your spirit? Where could I go to escape your presence? If I went up to heaven, you would be there. If I went down to the grave, you would be there too! If I could fly on the wings of the dawn, stopping to rest only on the far side of the ocean—even there your hand would guide me; even there your strong hand would hold me tight!"

Sing or listen to a favorite worship song or hymn.

Read aloud Romans 8:38-39: "I'm convinced that nothing can separate us from God's love in Christ Jesus our Lord: not death or life, not angels or rulers, not present things or future things, not powers or height or depth, or any other thing that is created."

Ask, "What is God's promise to us in these verses?" Celebrate that there is nothing that could happen today that could make God love us any more or less. God has only infinite love for all of us!

Ask for prayer requests. They can be anything—help for tests, friends who are ill, gratitude for teachers, and so on. Close by praying together, making sure each person gets an opportunity to pray aloud.

WE ARE THE LIGHT OF THE WORLD

Ask someone to read Psalm 9:1-2 aloud: "I will thank you, LORD, with all my heart; I will talk about your wonderful acts. I will celebrate and rejoice in you; I will sing praises to your name, Most High."

Sing or listen to a favorite worship song or hymn.

Read Matthew 5:13-16 aloud: "You are the salt of the earth. But if salt loses its saltiness, how will it become salty again? It is good for nothing except to be thrown away and trampled under people's feet. You are the light of the world. A city on top of a hill can't be hidden. Neither do people light a lamp and put it under a basket. Instead, they put it on top of a lampstand, and it shines on all who are in the house. In the same way, let your light shine before people, so they can see the good things you do and praise your Father who is in heaven."

Ask, "What does it mean to let your light shine? How can we let our lights shine today?" Brainstorm some ideas about how you can be a light and be sure to ask each other how it went at the end of the day.

Ask for prayer requests. They can be anything—help for tests, friends who are ill, gratitude for teachers, and so on. Close by praying together, making sure each person gets an opportunity to pray aloud.

MY HOPE IS IN THE LORD

Ask someone to read Psalm 25:4-5 aloud: "Make your ways known to me, LORD; teach me your paths. Lead me in your truth—teach it to me—because you are the God who saves me. I put my hope in you all day long."

Sing or listen to a favorite worship song or hymn.

Read aloud Romans 12:12: "Be happy in your hope, stand your ground when you're in trouble, and devote yourselves to prayer."

Affirm that you are devoting yourselves to prayer by gathering each morning for devotions. Say the verse together a few times to begin memorizing the passage.

Ask for prayer requests. They can be anything—help for tests, friends who are ill, gratitude for teachers, and so on. Close by praying together, making sure each person gets an opportunity to pray aloud.

SAVED FROM THE FIERY FURNACE

Ask someone to read Psalm 31:24 aloud: "All you who wait for the LORD, be strong and let your heart take courage."

Sing or listen to a favorite worship song or hymn.

Read aloud the story of Shadrach, Meshach, and Abednego from a storybook Bible. If you don't have a storybook Bible, read Daniel 3 from any Bible version.

Ask, "What is your favorite part of this story? How do you think Shadrach, Meshach, and Abednego were able to have such courage? When do we need courage?" Encourage the children to trust God to be with them and save them when they face trials.

Ask for prayer requests. They can be anything—help for tests, friends who are ill, gratitude for teachers, and so on. Close by praying together, making sure each person gets an opportunity to pray aloud.

CHAPTER
FOUR
Memorizing
Scriptures

Your word is a lamp before my feet
and a light for my journey.
—PSALM 119:105

R ecently I received a text message from a friend who had just dropped off her daughter for her freshman year in college. My friend was taking the long, lonely, twelve-hour drive home while already feeling a twinge of worry.

I'm a few years away from that situation, but as my kids grow, I'm becoming more and more aware that they are one day going to pack up their rooms and head out for adventures of their own. Along with all their stuff, they will take everything my husband and I taught them and all the experiences they had in our home, and they'll create their own lives.

Because this thought is always in the back of my mind, I am determined to be intentional about my family's prayer practices. My goal is to launch my children out into the world with firm spiritual habits, a hunger for God, and a deep desire for understanding God's word.

KNOWING THE STORY

As we prepare our kids for launch, I believe that one of the greatest gifts Christian parents can offer is knowledge of the grand story of God's redemption of the world. Sometimes, even with the best-laid plans, Sunday school lessons can dissolve into a history of Bible characters, a moral lesson,

55

or a complicated craft while leaving out the idea that every story in the Bible ultimately concerns God's love for the world. Kids may be able to recall the gist of a Bible story but completely miss the overarching story God has been telling since the beginning of time.

Of course we want our kids to know the stories of Bible heroes. Yes, we want our kids to discover the wisdom of biblical principles and moral lessons. We even want our kids to find some hands-on, real-life application in the scriptures. But most of all, we want our kids to discover that they are part of God's love story. The Bible isn't just a book we read sometimes and keep stored on a shelf. Instead, it is alive and active and speaking to us about who God is, what God has done, and what God is still doing in our lives.

MEMORIZING SCRIPTURES

When my kids outgrew the sing-along Bible memory CDs I kept in the minivan, we became complete failures at memorization. I had a good run with my older two as long as they could sing the verse while they recited it. If I asked them to simply speak the words of any of those verses, they'd be in big trouble!

I am 90 percent sure that my Bible verse memory block stems from a childhood tragedy when I got "excused" from the Bible quiz team because my friend and I were goofing off when we were supposed to be rehearsing answers. In my defense, she was squeezing my knee at the exact point that causes the trouble trifecta—the tickle giggle, the kick reflex, and the "That really hurts!" scream. To this day, my knee shudders when someone asks me a scripture reference or detail about a Bible story.

In spite of my troubled memory verse past, here is what I know to be true: God instructs us to write God's word on our hearts, to meditate on it day and night. It is important to God that we know not only the stories but also those verses that speak to us, through us, and for us when we lack the words to pray, praise, or even speak. Memorizing scriptures is not for the goal of winning competitions or conversations or even for a litany of moral takeaways but rather for the nourishment and encouragement of our hearts and the hearts of others. It helps form the spiritual foundation we stand on as we grow from children to adults, from young Christians to mature disciples.

LEARNING THE LANGUAGE OF PRAISE

Memorizing scripture also helps form a common prayer language—praise, lament, dependence on God, grace, hope, peace, and joy. In praying the scriptures we identify with the sadness of the Jobs and the Josephs and discover the joys of the Sarahs and the Marys. We speak our beliefs with the words of the scriptures when our hearts feel doubtful and uncertain. We claim the promises of God when the circumstances of our lives are shaky. And we pray the scriptures when we simply don't have the words ourselves.

HOW TO BEGIN SCRIPTURE MEMORY

Between my not-so-subtle switch from pasta noodles to spaghetti squash and my overly-complicated technology ticket reward system, my kids have to work to hide their groans and eye rolls at my new ideas and their implementation. As parents, I think we are all guilty of trying different techniques to inspire and motivate our children to adopt new and healthy habits. But here's one idea where we can encourage our children to voice their opinions and offer their help from the beginning. We can talk to our kids about how memorizing scripture helps us learn to pray and call on God in our times of need. We can ask them to choose a place to hang a decorative chalkboard or poster with a memory verse for each week. The kids can take turns writing the verses and/or drawing some pictures around the verse.

Choose a time each week when your family is home and unhurried. Gather around the Bible and read the verse aloud together. Challenge your kids not only to learn the words but also to pray the verse and ask God to speak through it. Explain that every time they walk by the board, they should stop and say the verse and repeat it to themselves throughout the day. You may want to add this to your family devotion time and recite the verse together each morning. I've included several great memory verses, but there are more than thirty thousand verses in the Bible. Feel free to add your favorites or ask your children for their favorites.

The LORD bless you and protect you.
—NUMBERS 6:24

"I've commanded you to be brave and strong, haven't
I? Don't be alarmed or terrified, because the LORD
your God is with you wherever you go."
—JOSHUA 1:9

God is our refuge and strength,
a help always near in times of great trouble.
—PSALM 46:1

LORD, listen closely and answer me,
because I am poor and in need.
Guard my life because I am faithful.
Save your servant who trusts in you—you! My God!
Have mercy on me, Lord,
because I cry out to you all day long.
—PSALM 86:1-3

Examine me, God! Look at my heart!
Put me to the test! Know my anxious thoughts!

Look to see if there is any idolatrous way in me,
then lead me on the eternal path!
—PSALM 139:23-24

"The LORD is good to everyone and everything;
God's compassion extends, to all his handiwork!"
—PSALM 145:9

God heals the brokenhearted
and bandages their wounds.
God counts the stars by number,
giving each one a name.
Our Lord is great and so strong!
God's knowledge can't be grasped!
—PSALM 147:35

Trust in the LORD with all your heart;
don't rely on your own intelligence.
—PROVERBS 3:5

I know the plans I have in mind for you, declares the
LORD; they are plans for peace, not disaster, to give
you a future filled with hope.
—JEREMIAH 29:11

Treat people in the same way that you want them to
treat you.
—LUKE 6:31

God so loved the world that he gave his only Son, so
that everyone who believes in him won't perish but will
have eternal life. God didn't send his Son into the world
to judge the world, but that the world might be saved
through him.
—JOHN 3:16-17

Don't let any foul words come out of your mouth.
Only say what is helpful when it is needed for building
up the community so that it benefits those who hear
what you say.
—EPHESIANS 4:29

Be kind, compassionate, and forgiving to each other, in
the same way God forgave you in Christ.
—EPHESIANS 4:32

Be glad in the Lord always! Again I say, be glad!
—PHILIPPIANS 4:4

I can endure all these things through the power of the
one who gives me strength.
—PHILIPPIANS 4:13

Jesus Christ is the same yesterday, today, and
forever!
—HEBREWS 13:8

We love because God first loved us.
—1 JOHN 4:19

CHAPTER FIVE

Prayers for Occasions

Rejoice always. Pray continually. Give thanks in every situation because this is God's will for you in Christ Jesus.
—1 THESSALONIANS 5:16-18

My pastor husband gladly performs his duty as the official pray-er for our congregation in any given situation. If he is there and something needs prayed for, you can bet that he will get called on. While some might get tired or annoyed at always being in the hot seat, he actually sees it as a privilege and welcomes the opportunity to bless people with prayers on any given occasion.

Lately members of the congregation have been moving into new houses and inviting my husband and me to pray and bless their homes. A few times we have taken our whole family for this ritual. We'll walk through each room of the house and pray together, inviting God to bless the home and the family and to use the home as a blessing for others. I've wondered, walking those rooms with my kids, what they must be thinking, what they make of such an experience. They read along and pray with us, and I think that something in them will remember these acts of prayer. They'll remember that some occasions require a special kind of prayer.

ORDINARY TIME PRAYERS

Some retired missionary friends of mine are absolute gifts that God wrapped up in a silver station wagon and sent to my driveway. They have stories of encouragement for any situation one could possibly go through and are quick to praise God for victories and blessings before I even recognize them in my life or in the lives of others. They are naturally given to prayer, and my spiritual life has been changed by their friendship. Whenever they take my kids out for a day with their children, my friends are sure to pause after buckling seatbelts to pray for the adventure to come—even before they leave the driveway! Let me just say that by the time I get my kids loaded into the van and ready to go anywhere, we should be in prayer—either confessing our ill thoughts or praising God for the miracle that we all made it to the car without incident.

But my wise friends have helped me teach my kids that prayer isn't reserved just for church, meals, or bedtime. We can prayer anywhere—even in the car! Now my kids often ask my husband or me to pray before a trip, for which I am so grateful.

THE INNER NUDGE TO PRAY

I dream that my kids will spontaneously pray in any situation, inviting God into their thoughts and actions throughout the day. I dream for them to pay attention to the inner nudge when they feel God inviting them into conversation or prayer for a friend in need or a word of praise at a sunset. I long for prayer to be the language of my family as we call upon God in special times, ordinary times, and all the in-between times.

Part of learning to pray continually is to stay open in prayer. Sometimes after we say amen, we check off prayer on our to-do list and shut down the conversation. But God has invited us—called us—to pray without ceasing, to keep the conversation going all day, every day. The hymn "What a Friend We Have in Jesus" is absolutely correct: "What a privilege to carry every thing to God in prayer!"

HOW TO USE THESE PRAYERS

The following prayers can be used when a specific situation calls for prayer. Prayer is appropriate on many occasions if only we had the words and the courage to say yes to our inner nudges. Hopefully we'll find confidence to speak words of prayer with our kids. The prayers are organized by theme, and I've also included some ideas for prayer stations that can help to form prayer habits at home.

PRAYERS FOR TRAVEL

Come, Lord Jesus, be our guide.
Lead us safely on our way.
Thank you for the view outside
And for our traveling company. Amen.

God who is with us here and there and along the way,
help us to look for you in everything. Grant us safe
travel and good conversation. Be blessed by our love for
you and for one another. Amen.

Loving God, we send out (name of person traveling)
today. We know that you are with us and with (name).
We know that there is nothing in this world that can
separate us from your love, and there is no place on
earth where you don't see us. We pray for traveling
mercies and for a safe return. Amen.

Go with us, God. You know the way.
Go with us, God. Give us strength for today.
Go with us, God. Shine bright in us.
Go with us, God. In you we place our hope and trust.
Amen.

PRAYERS DURING A TIME OF CHANGE

Change isn't always easy and doesn't always feel good,
Lord. But you are a God who never changes. You are
the same from generation to generation. When we face
change in our lives, help us to stand on the promise
that your love and affection for us will never change.
Give us peace and comfort, strength and courage to
stand on your promises today and always. Amen.

God, who is the same yesterday, today, and tomorrow,
hear our prayers as we feel the stress of change
stirring in our lives. Help us to remember that you are
writing your story in our lives no matter what happens.
You are the author of good things, and you promise to
give good gifts to your children. Help us not to worry
or be anxious but to lean on you and live in your love.
Amen.

PRAYERS OF CELEBRATION

—Birthdays—

Gracious God, we thank you for (name of the
birthday boy/girl) and we celebrate (him/her) today!

We praise you that you knit (him/her) together and you call (him/her) beloved. Make this a year of purpose, growth, discovery, and adventure so that we look back next year and praise you for your awesome work in (his/her) life. Amen.

Invite each person gathered to complete this one-line prayer: God, I thank you for (name of birthday boy/girl) because . . .

—Graduation—

God, we give you praise for your great work. We are thankful that you have given us so many reasons to bless your name. We celebrate that (name of graduate) has reached the goal of graduation. Schoolwork takes great effort and commitment, and you have encouraged and lifted up (name) every step of the way. Thank you for (his/her) dedication and persistence. We know that you have good things planned for (his/her) future. We celebrate today knowing that you are the God of our tomorrows. Walk behind, beside, and before us always. Amen.

PRAYERS FOR TIMES OF LOSS

—When a Family Member Dies—

Loving God, we don't always understand your timing,
but we trust that you are good. We know that you
hold us in your hands and wrap your love around us when
we are sad. We are sad today, Lord. Comfort us with
your presence. Grant us peace in our hearts. Fill our
minds with good memories of the one we love. You are
the great Healer, and we ask you to heal our hearts
today and wipe the tears from our eyes to see the
hope you have set before us. Amen.

—When a Pet Dies—

Loving and All-Comforting God, help our hearts to feel
better as we say good-bye to (name of pet). It is so
hard to imagine life without (name), but we know that
you heal broken hearts. Thank you for the memories
we shared, the joy (he/she) brought to our home, and
the fun we had together. We are grateful even in our
grief. Amen.

God of grace and mercy, we are struggling today. We don't understand, and we feel confused, betrayed, and scared. Help us to bring every feeling, every hurt, every fear, and all our tears to you and let you hold us. Help us to turn to you first for comfort, remembering that you offer healing to those who grieve. Amen.

PRAYER FOR MAKING TOUGH DECISIONS

God of wisdom, we have some touch choices ahead. You know the details of our situation. You know our hearts and have placed within us everything we need for this time and place. May we be wise with our words, our judgments, and our actions. Help us to act according to your will, seeking your guidance in every step. Grant us discerning minds to know the choice we need to make and give us grace as we seek your will. Amen.

PRAYER FOR HEALING

Healing God, we stand in need of healing—from sickness, brokenness, and those things that just don't feel right. Come with your healing presence, come with your love, come with your comfort, come with your wisdom, come with your grace. Come and heal, God. By the power of Jesus Christ and in his name, we pray for healing, knowing full well that you are able to accomplish more than we could ask or imagine. Come soon, Lord Jesus. Amen.

PRAYER FOR BACK TO SCHOOL

Summer is over, and it's time for school, Lord. Thank you for the rest and for the sunshine and for the family time. Thank you for the long nights and lazy mornings. As we enter another school year, we pray for our teachers and ask you to bless them beyond measure this year, Lord. We thank you for their love, wisdom, and generosity. Help us to be good students, to learn eagerly, to listen carefully, to help willingly, and to love unconditionally. We set this year before you and ask you to hold us all in your hands. Keep us safe from harm. Give us hearts and minds to hold what you have for us to learn this year. Amen.

PRAYER BEFORE TESTS

Lord, tests can cause stress, worry, and anxiety. May
we remember what we've learned and give our fears and
anxiety to you. Give us the peace of your calming
presence. Sit with us as we complete our test and
cheer us on to the end. Amen.

PRAYER OF GRATITUDE FOR FRIENDS

Loving God, we are so grateful that you created
friendship. You even call us friend! What a gift that
the Maker of the whole world is our very best friend.
And even still, you give us friends to play with, grow
with, learn from, share with, laugh with, eat with, love,
and be loved by. You truly are a good and wonderful
God. Thank you so much for our good friends. Help
us to treat others as we want to be treated. Help us
to forgive as you have forgiven us. Help us to love our
neighbors as ourselves. And help us to remember that a
friend loves at all times. We know these things because
you have taught us what it means to be a friend. Help
us share your friendship with others. Amen.

PRAYER STATIONS

Designate a place in your house where you will occasionally set out a few items to encourage prayer in the home. This will be your "Prayer Station." Explain to your family members that they may spend time at the prayer station whenever they feel led or are looking for something to do. The stations are meant to be informal opportunities for your family to make time to be in prayer.

Throw Your Cares

Set out small squares of paper and crayons. Place an open Bible nearby. Write 1 Peter 5:7 on an index card or whiteboard: "Throw all your anxiety onto him, because he cares about you."

When they ask, explain to your children that they can write down anything that makes them worried, anxious, or afraid. After they read the Bible verse, they should wad up the paper and toss it onto the open Bible as if they are throwing their anxiety into God's hands.

Spiritual Design

Cut out paper-doll figures from construction paper—think stick figures, not professional portraits! Cut out shirts, pants, and dresses that children can write on and dress the paper dolls. If you have younger children, write the various words from the scripture verse below on the clothes. Older kids can write the words on the clothes themselves.

Write Colossians 3:12-14 on an index card: "Therefore, as God's choice, holy and loved, put on **compassion**, **kindness**, **humility**, **gentleness**, and **patience**. Be tolerant with each other and, if someone has a complaint against anyone, forgive each other. As the Lord forgave you, so also forgive each other. And over all these things put on **love**, which is the perfect bond of unity."

Set out the verse, more construction paper, crayons, stickers, glue sticks, and safety scissors. Read the verse aloud and ask your children to "put on" the clothes on the paper dolls using glue. They can decorate the figures with words from the scriptures and with the other craft supplies. As they create, encourage them to put on these words—compassion, kindness, humility, gentleness, patience, and love—in their lives like they would put on clothing.

Advent Wreath

The first Sunday in Advent, set out an Advent wreath with four purple candles representing hope, love, joy, and peace, along with one white candle representing the birth of Jesus. Each Sunday, ask your children to help light the week's candle and invite God to teach them about hope, love, joy, or peace in the coming week.

Lenten Reflection

Set out a few small mirrors and an open Bible turned to John 3:16-17 with the verses highlighted. Invite your kids to read the Bible verses or read them aloud, replacing the words the world with their names. Encourage them to study their faces in the mirror and thank God for loving them so much that God would make a way for eternal life.

Anytime Prayers and Praises

Set out paper, pens, and crayons. When your kids need something to do, send them to the prayer station to pray by drawing pictures of what they are thankful for, in prayer about, or need help with. Encourage them to pray as they create and ask God to speak to them.

CHAPTER
SIX
Just for Parents
Prayers

Train children in the way they should go;
when they grow old, they won't depart from it.
—PROVERBS 22:6

Prayer matters to me. I want to set a pattern of prayer for my family that feels natural, real, and easy. Though it may be awkward for me to pray with my kids, I have no trouble finding words to pray for them in my private prayer time. I am often on my knees for them, pleading with God to protect them, help them, shine on them, and make me a better mother for them.

We pray for our kids because the Bible tells us to, but we mostly pray for our kids because we know that out of everything we can do for them, prayer may be the single most important act. We pray for our kids to build them up, to give them strength, to seek wisdom, and to protect them. Praying for our children is just as important as praying with them. It is part of building a spiritual foundation for them to stand on when they are older.

As parents, we have a profound impact on the spiritual lives of our kids. We not only teach them how to pray but also the importance of prayer by modeling the spiritual life for them. I don't try to put on a show for my kids, but neither do I hide from them that I read the Bible every day, write in my prayer journal, and spend focused time in prayer for my family, for the needs of the church, and for the world. They see their dad on the deck with his Bible and a cup of coffee.

They hear conversations about people who suffer and our intercessory prayers for them. My husband and I model lives of prayer so that our children know what it looks like.

Before I knew better, I thought that a committed prayer life meant spending hours in completely focused prayer. But now I know that a commitment to a life of prayer means praying all the time, without ceasing, letting the prayers come in and out just as I breathe. The conversation with God does not end when we say amen. Instead, our prayers continue on with every breath—gratitude, help, awe. I love Anne Lamott who named a book after her three favorite prayers: *Help, Thanks, Wow.* That's how I teach my kids to pray: being mindful of God's presence and provision in all things and naming their gratitude, dependence, and awe in every moment.

While children are young, we may not be sure what will stick with them. But we hope that through our witness they will understand the importance and the gift of a life of prayer as they grow older and discover which actions will become habits.

PRAYING THE SCRIPTURES FOR OUR KIDS

In the same way that we memorize scripture verses together as a family as a way to pray through scripture, we can pray the scriptures for our kids. So many verses lend themselves to replacing a name with our kids' names and claiming a scriptural truth for them. If we are unsure how to begin praying for our kids, we can start by praying scriptures for them. Here are a few examples:

"Create a clean heart for (child's name), God; put a new, faithful spirit deep inside (name)!" (adapted from Ps. 51:10).

"Help (child's name) to be strong and fearless. Don't let (him/her) be afraid and scared by (his/her) enemies, because the Lᴏʀᴅ is the one who marches with (name). You won't let (him/her) down or abandon (him/her)" (adapted from Deut. 31:6).

"Help (child's name) to be kind, compassionate, and forgiving to others, in the same way God forgave (name) in Christ" (adapted from Eph. 4:32).

HOW TO BEGIN PRAYING FOR OUR KIDS

Almost every suggestion and activity in this book requires a change of habit. In order to make prayer a priority in our lives, we have to create some space or margin. We must slow down a bit, say no to some things, get enough sleep, and make choices that demonstrate what is really important to us. To create a habit of prayer for our kids and our families, we have to look at our daily schedules and find the time. If we don't find time in our current schedules, we should consider what we can cut out or move around to gain ten minutes of personal time to spend in prayer. And probably the most important step for busy parents—we should write the prayer time on our calendars. If we make prayer time a part of the day's activities, we won't forget, get too tired, or find something else to fill that time.

Because I have four kids and a husband who are different and equally awesome in their own ways, I sometimes draw five squares on a journal page and write all my prayers for each of them in the spaces. That way I spend concentrated time praying for each of them. Whenever and however I do it, I see a huge change in my family dynamic as I witness God answering my prayers.

What follows are some prayers to get you started, but feel free to simply talk to God about your kids. What are you worried about? What needs do they have? What do you love about them? What are they teaching you about God's love?

God of love and grace, I thank you for my sweet kids. They teach me so much about your forgiveness and your patience. Refine me and make me more like you. Give me eyes to see my kids the way you do: with compassion, love, and kindness. When they fail, give me patience to grant grace and love. When they win, grant me the energy to celebrate with them. When they need me, offer me the wisdom to stop what I'm doing and give them my time. When they are hurting, may I have comforting arms to hold them and the right words to console them. You know them well; you made them. You know me well; you made me. Come and be the center of our family. We are yours. Amen.

God of all our years, my kids are growing fast. The early days were long and difficult, but these later years are going by too quickly. Help me to savor experiences with these sweet babies. Help me not to wish away the long days but to lean into you and your strength. Forgive me when I fall short of who you made me to be. Give me second, third, and fourth chances by your grace. Bind my heart to yours in love and be the center of my life. Amen.

Help my kids choose to follow after you, O Lord. May the example I set and the habits I embrace set a strong spiritual foundation. Set your love like a seal on their hearts. Plant your word like a seed in their souls. Be their God and seek them if they turn away. I depend on you for everything, Lord. I give my family to you in trust and in hope. Let your will be done in us as a family. Make us yours. Amen.

Thank you, Lord, for my amazing family. Thank you for each of my kids who are gifts, every one. Thank you for their laughter, their innocence, their childlike faith, their quickness to trust, their spirit of adventure, and their zeal for life. Teach me about who you are and who I am by our shared leadership in their lives. Help me train them when they are young and let them go when they grow up. You are a good and beautiful God, and I am ever grateful for your many blessings. Amen.

Don't let anyone look down on you because you are young.
Instead, set an example for the believers.
—1 TIMOTHY 4:12

As I mentioned before, our homes are like little house churches where parents serve as pastors, chaplains, and Christian educators. Because of this, part of making disciples of our kids is teaching them to pray on their own. Even at a young age, kids can develop the habit of lifting their prayers to God, praying for others, and listening to God's voice. We can point them to the habit when they are afraid, worried, or simply bored.

One of the best ways for kids to develop personal prayer habits is with a prayer journal. It doesn't have to be fancy, just a notebook will do. Before they can write, teach kids to draw pictures of what they want to pray about. Oftentimes they will draw the family members or the family pet. They are learning to bring those they love to God in prayer.

Once children know how to write, encourage them to make four squares on the page and make four lists: Praises, I'm Sorry, For Others, My Hopes. Encourage them to reflect on each prayer theme and make a list of praises, things for which they are sorry, prayers for others, and things they hope for in their own lives. Ask them to read these lists aloud as a prayer to God and refer back to previous pages to note answered prayers.

For older kids or kids who love to write, prompt them to write letters to God during their prayer time. They should write like they are writing to a friend—celebrating all that has happened, sharing needs, hopes and dreams, prayers for others. Again, be sure to have them look back every now and then to see the ways in which God has heard and answered their prayers.

KIDS PRAYING FOR KIDS

At our church on Wednesday nights, the kids break up into their small groups to share prayer requests and pray together. I am always amazed at the vulnerability with which these kids share their hearts. They lay it all out there for one another and the kids take it as a privilege and a challenge to pray for each other. It's an amazing thing to be a part of. On Thursday mornings at our morning devotion table, my kids will make sure their friends are on our family prayer list as we pray together. They hear, take seriously, and commit to pray for one another!

I am sure that our church is not the only one whose kids have taken prayer seriously. This image of kids praying for kids is one way we see our prayer habits coming back to us—we see them sticking when our kids volunteer to pray for a friend or make sure our family prays for a friend who is struggling. It is another indication that the spiritual foundation is being formed and shaped into something they'll be able to stand on.

PERSONAL PRAYER TIME FOR KIDS

As you carve out time in your own schedule for personal prayer time, think about moments in the day when your kids might find some time, maybe right when they wake up, right before bed, or during snack time after school. Create some scenarios for them—having quiet time on the back porch, sitting at the kitchen table with the lamp just before bedtime, hiding in the closet with a flashlight. Get them excited about personal space and quiet time and let them pick out a notebook to be their prayer journal. Encourage them to decorate it or get a cool pen or pencil to write with.

Because they are just beginning to develop the habit, they'll need reminders and encouragement, but don't we all? Invite them to ask you if you've had your personal prayer time as well and hold each other accountability to making prayer a regular part of daily life.

ACTS PRAYER

Adoration: I praise you because...
Confession: I confess that...
Thanksgiving: I'm thankful for...
Supplication: Please help...

QUESTIONING PRAYER

I wonder how...
I wonder why...
I wonder when...
I wonder if...
I wonder who...

WRITING LETTERS TO GOD

Dear God, I am thankful that...
Today was...
I felt your presence when...
...needs your healing/comfort/grace today.
Help me to...
I will give you all the praise. In Jesus' name. Amen.

PRAYER LISTS
Make a list of things to lift up to the Lord.

Praises   I'm Sorry   For Others   My Hopes

A DAILY PRAYER
In the morning when I rise
And lift my eyes to see the day,
Help me, Lord, to look for you.

In the day when I am rushed
Or tired from the work,
Help me, Lord, to look for you.

In the night when I am home
And gathered with my family,
Help me, Lord, to look for you.

In my sleep when I'm at rest
And my imagination runs wild and free,
Help me, Lord, to look for you. Amen.

CLOSING THOUGHTS

Pray like this:
Our Father who is in heaven,
uphold the holiness of your name.
Bring in your kingdom
so that your will is done on earth as it's done in heaven.
Give us the bread we need for today.
Forgive us for the ways we have wronged you,
just as we also forgive those who have wronged us.
And don't lead us into temptation,
but rescue us from the evil one.
—MATTHEW 6:9-13

What greater gift can I give my children than to point them in the direction of their Creator? Of all the tasks, to-dos, expectations, and priorities of parenting, the greatest among them is to train my kids in the way of Jesus—the one who taught us to pray, the one who showed us the way to the Father, the one who stands at the ready with open arms and open ears to hear our prayers.

I don't want my kids to pray because I make them or because their father is the pastor and they have to. I want them to love time with God, to crave time with God, to seek

God's wisdom, strength, courage, joy, and peace. That's my goal. We don't pray together as a family for achievement of a goal. We pray because otherwise our family would be a moving circus in a minivan. Instead, we are fully aware of God's love and grace that surrounds us, and we want to sit smack dab in the middle of it.

PRAY LIKE THIS

Recently at a children's ministry party my husband and I held at the parsonage, I asked one of the kids to pray for our meal. The eight-year-old girl beamed with pride and took the task very seriously. She looked around to make sure everyone was duly reverent, and then she declared, "Let us pray." You would have thought that she was about to lead a boisterous, extemporaneous prayer that would take us all straight to the throne of God. She stood tall, took a deep breath, and in her best preacher voice she began, "Our Father who art in heaven, hallowed be Thy name . . . ."

Everyone joined in and prayed along. The adults in the room giggled, but she was doing what she had learned. I have a hunch that she had in mind to pray a blessing for the meal but then panicked and started The Lord's Prayer instead. But I love that she demonstrated her practice of prayer. She has prayed that prayer her whole life, and so it has become her prayer language. She was asked to pray and that is what came out. Jesus said, "Pray like this" so that's what she did.

Everyone at the party that day saw the girl's commitment to prayer. A prayer she had heard all her life really sunk in! We see our kids grow in faith by the choices they make, the prayers they offer, and the leadership roles they gladly accept. We only see glimpses here and there, but their growth is evident if we look for it.

I hope that you have been encouraged and inspired to make family prayer time a priority in your home. I hope you found an idea or two that will work for your family. I will pray for you as you seek God with your family, and I ask you to pray for me as well. May God be glorified by families who serve the Lord by gathering together in prayer, Bible study, and worship. And may you find that "God will meet your every need out of his riches in the glory that is found in Christ Jesus" (Phil. 4:19).

NOTES

1. This prayer is widely attributed to Ralph Waldo Emerson, but in fact the author is unknown. The prayer has been printed in hymnals and published alone as *Father, We Thank You* (New York: SeaStar Books, 2000).

2. For more prayer ideas, see Kara Lassen Oliver's book *Passing It On: How to Nurture Your Children's Faith Season by Season* (Nashville, TN: Upper Room Books, 2015).

3. Robert Van De Weyer, *Celtic Prayers* (Nashville, TN: Abingdon Press, 1997), 27.

4. George Barna, *Transforming Children into Spiritual Champions: Why Children Should Be Your Church's #1 Priority* (Grand Rapids, MI: Baker Books, 2003), 58.

5. Beverly Burton and Drew Dyson, *Soul Tending: Life Forming Practices for Older Youth and Young Adults* (Nashville, TN: Abingdon Press, 2002), 7.

CPSIA information can be obtained
at www.ICGtesting.com
Printed in the USA
FSOW04n0019100316
17858FS